COMMON SENSE REDISCOVERED:

LESSONS FROM THE TERRORIST ATTACK ON AMERICA

Dale M. Herder

COMMON SENSE REDISCOVERED: LESSONS FROM THE
TERRORIST ATTACK ON AMERICA

ISBN 0-9753024-0-X

Library Of Congress Control Number: 2004093511

DMH and Associates, Publisher

Printed by Mercury Print Productions, Inc., Rochester, N.Y.

Dedicated to Todd Beamer and the other brave men and women who fought back against the terrorists who had hijacked their flight, United 93, on September 11, 2001.

We have just begun to appreciate the wisdom, decisiveness, and courage of Todd Beamer and his fellow passengers.

May we all be as wise, decisive, and courageous in the current crisis.

Acknowledgements

For reading this study and making editorial suggestions, I thank the following friends and colleagues on both sides of the Atlantic and Pacific Oceans (and on both sides of the liberal-conservative divide in the United States):

Robert M. LaFollette III, and Lou E. LaFollette
William Morley and Virginia Morley
Diane M. Herder

Prof.-Dr. Wolfgang Blumbach
Dr. John Hinchcliff

Gustave Breymann
John Duley
Rev. James Kocher
William Ruddock
Dr. Dan C. Wertz

Dale M. Herder
May 2004

Table of Contents

Foreword

Chapter I   Thomas Paine and *Common*   *13*
             Sense in 1776 and 2001

Chapter II   Understanding the Terrorists   25
             and the 9/11 Attack

Chapter III Ten Lessons That Can Lead   59
             to Action

   Lesson 1   America's Ideals and   62
               Morality ARE America

   Lesson 2   No Sleeping On Watch   67

   Lesson 3   We Will Have to Absorb   71
               Future Hits

   Lesson 4   We Must Decide Whether   73
               Oil and Israel Are Enough
               to Keep Us in the Middle East

Lesson 5	Fix the U.S. Immigration and Naturalization Service	76
Lesson 6	Citizens Must Continue to Tell It Like It Is	80
Lesson 7	Three Things Are Needed to Treat the New Global Cancer: Power, Morality, and Allies	82
Lesson 8	Keep Our Press Free	87
Lesson 9	Invite and Expect American Muslims to Assimilate	88
Lesson 10	The United States Must Earn (Not Assume As A Right) Its Leadership Position in the World	90
Conclusion	Concluding Comments Aboard a Doomed Airliner	95

FOREWORD

This is a sequel to Thomas Paine's pamphlet, *Common Sense*, which was published in 1776.

The purpose of this treatise is to tell the truth and prompt thought after the Islamic terrorist attack on the United States on September 11, 2001. The author is unfettered by debt to any political, social, economic, or religious organization, and he does not advocate the ideology of any such group.

The conclusion to this book calls for action by the reader, and the ten lessons in Chapter III suggest what action is needed if liberty is to be secured for mankind.

These are the times that try men's souls. The summer soldier and the sunshine patriot will, in this crisis, shrink from the service of their country; but he that stands it now deserves the love and thanks of man and woman. . . .What we obtain too cheap, we esteem too lightly; it is dearness only that gives everything its value. Heaven knows how to put a proper price upon its goods; and it would be strange indeed, if so celestial an article as *Freedom* should not be highly rated.

Thomas Paine, *The American Crisis*, no. 1 [December 23, 1776]

Chapter I

Thomas Paine and *Common Sense* in 1776 and 2001

They hit us right between the eyes.

Nearly three thousand souls were hurled into eternity at the hands of nineteen Islamic fanatics who butchered them on our own soil. The terrorists took careful aim, and our airplanes became their fangs.

We reacted from our guts and from our heads on September 11, 2001, but we missed an opportunity to grab the steering wheel. We did not seize the moment and define the personal and collective sacrifice it was our duty to make as a tribute to the symbolic Americans who had died in our place.

What should we have said and done? When asked by news reporters what we should do in response to the attack, President George W. Bush said, in so many words, "Get on with our lives; shop, go to Disney World, go about our business as usual. Don't let the terrorists think they have made us prisoners of fear."

He meant well, but he could have done better. The rest of us meant well, too, but we should have done better.

We were in shock, and we did the best we could. We were brave, resolved, and temperate. But by sliding back into "normality" so quickly, we ducked a challenge to our national and individual morality.

On October 16, 2001, just four weeks after the attack, Bill Moyers said well what we all need yet to act upon: "We're survivors, you and I. We will be defined not by the lives we led until the 11th of September, but by the lives we will lead from now on."

Each death on 9/11 was a moral call. Each death beckons us to give more than the money we so generously lavished on the Red Cross after the attack.

This slim book is an echo to the CALL TO ACTION AND SACRIFICE that Thomas Paine sent throughout the American colonies in 1776, when he published his pamphlet, *Common Sense*. In that little booklet, Paine proposed that Americans STOP conducting business as usual. He pricked his fellow colonists and prompted them to action in order to save their ideals and the new nation they were building.

The British wolf was at the door in 1776.

The Islamic terrorist wolf came calling in 2001.

By rediscovering *Common Sense*, let us call to action, this time, more than just Americans. This is a summons to ALL who believe that life, liberty, and the pursuit of happiness are the natural rights of mankind everywhere.

What the United States and the free world does now, as we face a new breed of fanatics, will be writ large in future chapters of human progress--or misery. If we are wise, we will interpret the 9/11 attack as an opportunity.

This is not a time to remain seated.

A Quick Refresher in American History

Who was Thomas Paine, and what was the pamphlet he wrote in the birthing room of America?

Thomas Paine was a free-thinking Englishman who came to the American colonies on the eve of the American Revolution. He accepted a job in the bookstore of Robert Aitkin, in Philadelphia, and in early 1775 he met a bright young physician, Dr. Benjamin Rush, in that bookstore. Benjamin Rush was another freethinker—and a man of action.

Dr. Rush had read an anti-slavery article written by Paine, so he knew the sharpness of the young

Englishman's pen. Rush himself wanted to write an argument in favor of independence, but he feared the consequences. He remembered well what had happened earlier, when he had written a strong article supporting the abolition of slavery: Many of his patients had left him.

Independence was not a popular cause in the American colonies as late as 1775. Only about a third of the American colonists were bold enough to support the idea of immediate independence, a complete separation from Mother England. Another third were fence-sitters who were waiting to see which way the wind would blow. The final third were loyal British subjects who were totally opposed to independence.

In light of his previous loss of patients, and in light of the two thirds of the colonial population who were NOT eager for revolution, Dr. Rush realized that he was not the best person to publicly advocate for separation. Still determined to stir the pot, however, he realized that young Paine had no business or reputation to lose. And Rush knew that the time was precisely right to move the fence-sitters and naysayers. Perhaps Paine, who had arrived from England a year earlier with letters of introduction from Benjamin Franklin, was the man who could bring the pot to a boil.

Dr. Rush urged Paine to write a pamphlet that could change people's minds. Paine accepted Rush's challenge, and he wrote *Common Sense,* a treatise that appeared, in its first printing, as an anonymous pamphlet in Philadelphia on January 10, 1776.

It snapped its readers to full alert. " We were blind, but on reading these enlightening words the scales have fallen from our eyes," averred one Connecticut colonist.

What Paine said about common sense MADE SENSE. His words were clear. His sentences were crisp. His arguments were powerfully short, direct, and persuasive. He was a brilliant teacher, and his course of study could have been called "Elementary Principles of Democracy."

Paine's preferred title for the pamphlet was "Plain Truth," but Dr. Rush convinced him to call it "Common Sense." Average people could pick up *Common Sense* and read it in one sitting (or have it read to them quickly by a literate spouse or friend).

The booklet was more than a quick read: It stuck in the eyes, ears, and imaginations of colonists--and soldiers in the Revolutionary Army as they retreated up the Island of Manhattan and across the Hudson River into New Jersey. The pamphlet's readership spread up and down the East Coast of the New World.

Everyone wanted a copy, and nearly everyone had it, dog-eared, in his pocket.

Plain and compelling arguments such as the following convinced the uncommitted and the doubters that the time had come for total separation from England:

> *The cause of America is in a great measure the cause of all mankind. . . .*
>
> *To say they will never (attack us) again is idle. . . .*
>
> *A French bastard landing with an armed banditti, and establishing himself king of England against the consent of the natives, is in plain terms a very paltry rascally original.—It certainly hath no divinity in it. However, it is needless to spend much time in exposing the folly of hereditary right; if there are any so weak as to believe it, let them promiscuously worship the ass and lion, and welcome. I shall neither copy their humility, nor disturb their devotion.*
>
> *In the following pages I offer nothing more than simple facts, plain arguments, and common sense; and have no other preliminaries to settle with the reader, than that he will divest himself of prejudice and prepossession, and suffer his reason and his feelings to determine for themselves . . . and generously enlarge his views beyond the present day.*

The sun never shined on a cause of greater worth. 'Tis not the affair of a city, a country, a province, or a kingdom, but of a continent . . . 'Tis not the concern of a day, a year, or an age; posterity are virtually involved in the contest, and we will be more or less affected, even to the end of time, by the proceedings now. Now is the seed-time. . . .

I mean not to exhibit horror for the purpose of provoking revenge, but to awaken us from the fatal and unmanly slumbers, that we may pursue determinately some fixed object.

For myself, I fully and conscientiously believe, that it is the will of the Almighty, that there should be diversity of religious opinions among us. . . .

But where, says some, is the King of America? I'll tell you . . . in America THE LAW IS KING. For as in absolute governments the King is law, so in free countries the law ought to be King; and there ought to be no other.

O ye that love mankind! Ye that dare oppose, not only the tyranny, but the tyrant, stand forth! Every spot of the old world is overrun with oppression. Freedom hath been hunted round the globe. Asia, and Africa, have long expelled her—Europe regards her like a stranger, and England hath given her warning to depart. O! receive the fugitive, and prepare in time an asylum for mankind.

Thomas Paine made it clear that Americans needed to be fully awake. They needed to prick up their ears to small sounds in the cellar. Termites ignored too long can undergo metamorphosis, move out of the cellar, and become the wolf at the door.

The Situation Today

As these words are being written, in the first month of the year 2002, we are faced with foreign and domestic termites that have chewed through a major timber under the common hopes and aspirations of mankind. The September 11, 2001, terrorist attack on New York City and Washington took place just three months ago.

To say that the enemy will never attempt another attack on us is, to use Paine's word, "idle." We have solid reason to expect more attacks, and it is likely that some of them will be biological, chemical, nuclear— and, worst of all, cyber assaults that can shut down our electrical, communication, banking, transportation, and health support systems.

"Sleepers" are at this moment lying in wait in the United States, Canada, and European nations, as well as in Somalia, Sudan, Yemen, the Philippines, Malaysia, Indonesia, and other places around the world. When they determine that the time is right, or when they are called by their co-religionists to act, they will strike at people around the world whom the fanatics call "the Infidel."

Chief among the targets will be, once again, Americans on American soil, since we have inherited the former European mantle of "crusaders" in the minds of the Islamic terrorists. (This is ironic, since the United States is more officially secular than any European nation, and the population of the United States is more religiously and peacefully diverse than any nation in the world.)

Many Islamic fundamentalists and terrorists still think the same thoughts their ancestors contemplated ten centuries ago. Furthermore, they feel as threatened by television, the Internet, and democracy as their ancestors did by the European Christians who marched across Europe and Eurasia in order to attack the Muslims whom THEY saw as the Infidel.

Unfortunately, many Moslems overseas think Americans dislike or hate Islam. The truth is that most Americans know LITTLE about Islam. Therefore, most Americans have not held negative feelings toward Moslems in the past.

The September 11 attack on the United States has caused more and more Americans to BECOME aware of Islam—and many Americans now are forming their first opinion ever of this religion. Unfortunately for the vast majority of decent, intelligent, and peace-loving Moslems around the globe, Americans and citizens of hundreds of nations now are developing a

PROFOUNDLY NEGATIVE opinion of Mohammed, his teachings, and his followers. The 9/11 fanatics and other jihadists should be blamed for creating this negative opinion of their religion.

Because of political correctness, most Americans are not saying out loud what they really think about Islam since the 9/11 attack. They are shutting their mouths except in conversations with close friends, but their minds are silently convinced: Islam is failing its followers.

The fanatics' assault on the World Trade Center and the Pentagon was watched on television around the world as it actually happened or in instant replays. The attack is the single most common and simultaneously shared event in human history, and it therefore has become the most compelling negative advertisement for any religion in the history of the world.

It is probable that no new attack on the United States has taken place since September 11, 2001, because hundreds of sleepers are in custody in the U.S. and in nations around the world. Many now are being deported from the United States and other Western nations, and thousands more should be sent packing without delay for having overstayed their welcome in the lands of the free and tolerant.

Despite the threat we still face from the fanatics, time is on the side of the free world, and we can move with a deliberateness that would unnerve a cheetah.

Tongues of defectors are wagging, and tongues of wolves will loosen in Islamic enclaves such as Dearborn, Michigan; Hamburg, Germany; and Milan, Italy. More sleepers will be caught, and we will capture their notes and computer hard drives. Eventually, many of them will recognize the folly of fighting for a cause that shackles the human mind and cripples the natural human desire for progress.

But turning the tide will require determination and grit that seems to be rare in modern Americans and other Westerners who have lived a life of plenty. Have we lost our collective memory of what it means to struggle? Are we unwilling to absorb losses in order to achieve what is noble and right? Have we lost our instinct and will to survive a wolf attack?

If we are honest about the state of the American nation, and the state of the West, we must face the very real possibility that the greatest threat to our freedom might be our desire for immediate gratification, our greed, our hubris, and our ignorance about our democratic roots. Maybe the termites in our cellar are mostly homegrown, and maybe they have prompted unusual ferociousness in the foreign termites beside them who are swooning in the stink of our arrogance and hollow materialism.

Less than a month before the birth of the United States in 1776, John Adams wrote to Patrick Henry and said, "the decree has gone forth, and it cannot be recalled, that a more equal liberty than had prevailed in other parts of the earth must be established in America."

Do we still believe deeply in such ideals?   Are we willing to die, if necessary, to preserve the more equal liberty that now exists in more places than ever?

Must more innocent people suffer the horror of another 9/11 attack before we in the West realize that we are at war?

Are we CAPABLE of understanding that there are human wolves in the world, and that they howl nightly around their tribal campfires as they lust for our blood?

Chapter II

Understanding the Terrorists and the 9/11 Attack

What is the nature of the Islamic fanatic, and why is he determined to destroy the underpinnings of Western Civilization?

As stated earlier, the Islamic fanatic has a worldview that is ancient.

He missed the European Enlightenment, and he neither understands nor shares the results of the eighteenth-century mental awakening that we inherited in the West. The culture of the fanatics who attacked us is many miles—and many centuries—removed from our view of the world. It also is eons away from our scientific achievements and our constitutional freedoms.

Most of all, it is lifetime away from HOPE.

We in the West undervalue hope. Few of us understand that it is the magnet to a better future. Fewer still understand that engaging in hope leads to mental illness in dozens of nations around our planet. For millions of people, hope is a kind of psychosis, like delusions of grandeur or clinical depression.

The 9/11 kamikazes are incapable of thinking, as we do in the West every minute of every day, that a better future for mankind can be CREATED by using Reason and a form of governance based on a balance of powers. Because of our open and inquiring worldview, and because of hope, we are taught in our schools and homes to question and speak out. Most Islamic fundamentalists, on the other hand, are taught never to question and never to speak out, since everything is in the hands of Allah, or fate, or tribal chieftans.

Like the serf in Europe during the Dark Ages, the common Islamic fundamentalist has few choices in life. He learns the hard way, if he is not smart, that it is best to simply obey.

If he wishes to keep his hands and legs--and head--it is best to shut his mouth, smile into every TV camera, and pray for a better life in Paradise when death finally releases him from the misery of this existence.

To understand the nature of the men who attacked us in New York and Washington, D.C., we must remember two things: 1.) It is a short step from misery and hopelessness to suicide and martyrdom, and 2.)

The Enlightenment never released the terrorists from misery and hopelessness.

In addition to their twisted interpretation of the Koran, there appear to be three primary reasons why the fanatics attacked the United States on September 11, 2001:

1. **They are jealous** of the educational and technological leadership of the West

2. **They are frightened** to change from their past-oriented and absolute world, and to enter the modern era

3. **They are angry** and fed up with Western (especially American) double-talk and support of their ancient enemies, the Jews

Jealousy

Whether one likes the West or not, it is foolish to deny its influence around the globe. Many Islamic fanatics, in their downward spiral into poverty, in their sense of alienation, and in their massive unemployment, are deeply envious of the West. This envy has become even more bitter and evident in the past two decades as more and more people in the Middle East, Southeast Asia, and Africa have gained access to television and Internet computer images that portray the rich lifestyle and productive jobs in the West.

Most of what Islamic terrorist culture has seen on television has been the MATERIAL wealth of people in the West. Unfortunately, this one-eyed view of Western Civilization lacks depth, and it has made the jealousy gap wider than religion alone would have created.

Poor, hopeless, and desperate people in the Middle East look at the one or two TV sets in some of their villages and ask questions that would never occur to us:

"What and where is this world in which people all have toilets and hot water and automobiles and straight teeth and the freedom to marry whomever they wish?

What and where is such an utterly unbelievable place in which women can go to school side-by-side with men, people can think and say what they believe, people can tell their tribal chieftan what to do, and people truly worry about avoiding fat and salt in their food?

Is it even possible that such a place exists where people who are poor are nearly all overweight?

Like the men and women who lived behind the Iron Curtain during the Cold War, many Islamic zealots feel deprived and cheated. As my friend, Professor Givi Janjgava, told me in 1992, during my first visit to the former Soviet Republic of Georgia during its civil war against its Osetian and Abkhazi tribes, "Life is unfair because we are born only once—and we had the misfortune of being born in the Soviet Union."

Fear

Many Islamic fundamentalists, and the terrorists especially, are frightened of the West's encroachment onto their lands and into their values. They worry when they see more and more oil men in their cities and more sexually explicit television, films, CD's, and musical icons influencing their children.

More important, they fear the inevitable confrontation they must have with *themselves and their own culture*. They are running from two questions: "What is it in our culture that holds us back?" and "Why are we willing to live as slaves?"

In 1698, Algernon Sidney, one of the fathers of Western democracy, said, "All the Kingdoms of the Arabians, Medes, Persians, Moors, and others of the East are . . . wanting that wisdom and valour which is requir'd for the institution of a good Government, they languish in perpetual slavery, and propose to themselves nothing better than to live under a gentle Master, which is but a precarious life, and little to be valued by men of bravery and spirit."

Algernon Sidney's 300-year-old comment above might provide the answer to the question the fanatics fear most.

Anger

The Islamic fundamentalists "read between the lines" every time the West backs absolutist governments such as the former Shah of Iran or the Saud Family in Saudi, Arabia. We are perceived as inconsistent and unfair as we shift our support in the Arab world and buy "friendship." Isn't it true, as much as we in the West hate to admit it, that we have traded low oil prices for our approval (or acceptance) of royal and dictatorial corruption in the Middle East?

And isn't it true, as much as we in the West are reluctant to talk about it, that we respond to powerful Israeli political and financial interests in the United States Congress by unhesitatingly giving enormous military support and billions of dollars to Israel every year? When have we been serious AND CREDIBLE about creating an independent Palestinian state in the Middle East?

The hatred between Islam and Judaism is over two thousand years old, and the United States has allowed itself to be drawn into the middle of this ancient blood feud for two reasons: Our need for oil and our close alliance with Israel since its establishment in 1948. From the perspective of conservative Sharia (Islamic law), which guides fundamentalist Islamic leaders as they "read between the lines," Americans are favoring Jewish Israelis over Islamic Palestinians.

Viewed through the lens of Sharia, Westerners (especially Americans) lack virtue. Fanatics see us backing the wrong people and the wrong religions, and therefore they see us as filthy infidels and a death-deserving foe.

Terrorist leaders smile as Westerners preach about human rights and democratic ideals.

They have cause to smile, for it is clear that our preaching is not saving Western culture and Western societies from internal rot. The terrorists point out examples. Americans sing hymns to their king, the Rule of Law, but there seem to be other kings in America and the West. Huge corporations are able to influence Congress and help certain politicians "buy" elections.

Americans sing hymns to their free press, but news in the American media has become entertainment. The news "industry" is owned by Disney, Incorporated; Westinghouse Corporation; AOL Time-Warner, and other conglomerates that are interested in TV ratings and end-of-quarter stock profits, rather than intelligent analysis and balanced news reportage that will keep a government honest.

It is not difficult for the fanatics to point out other examples. Rich American corporations such as ENRON and WORLDCOM and TYCO rape their employees financially, children take guns to school, thousands of priests have molested children in their churches, and parents inject heroin into the arms of their children and neighbor children to teach them how to use drugs. Husbands and wives boast on television about committing adultery, fathers do not support their children, and convicted prisoners get heart transplants that hard-working citizens cannot afford. The West's out-of-wedlock birth rates and television shows exhibiting nude women and sexually explicit behavior are seen as decadent, corrupt, destructive of children, and good reason for anger and derision by people who interpret the Koran literally and conservatively.

Unfortunately, BBC, CNN, and the Sky Channel satellites are feeding and helping to create these negative impressions of America and the West.

In every country this author has visited throughout Europe, the Middle East, Asia, Southeast Asia, and Oceania, television news and entertainment programs reflect the *worst* of American culture. The international TV audience sees America through images of drive-by shootings, armed guards in our school buildings, drug busts, M-TV, vapid soap operas, old films featuring gangsters and machine guns, and new films featuring Rambo and the Terminator.

Americans frequently are described by thoughtful people around the world as not only friendly, open and generous, but also rich, wasteful, materialistic, naïve, poorly educated, loud, and incapable of speaking or writing their own language well.

Little is shown on international TV about American research and achievements in medicine, agriculture, and astrophysics.

Little is shown or known about our willingness to openly debate and do something to improve opportunities for handicappers, women, and minorities.

Little is shown or known about the fact that a poor man (and soon a woman) can become president in the United States.

Little is shown or known about the genuine decency of the hard-working American men and women who continue to feed and provide stability for much of the world.

Hollow Promises and An Alternative In The Islamic Terrorist World

By striking at the West out of fanatical religious belief, jealousy, fear, and anger, and by promising their suicidal young men a moronic but attractive eternity with a bevy of virgins in paradise, the terrorist leaders have misled and betrayed their emasculated young males. The mullahs, imams, warlords, and family patriarchs who are exploiting the Palestinian cause and splattering the blood and brains of their young people, are doing so to relieve their own frustration and fear.

At the same time, they are making it appear to their desperate young men that they finally *can* become men, and they are tricking them into believing that only their tragic suicides will give their lives purpose.

By avoiding change, fundamentalist Islamic leaders are stopping some of their people from participating in the West's "decadent morality"—but at the same time they are preventing their followers from joining the modern world of growing human freedom. Treat women as equals of men? Face the competition of women who are educated to serve as lawyers, judges, and government officials?

A small number of the Islamic men in charge will do anything to avoid facing the above questions. They know they are not on the wave of progress that is cresting in the direction of reason and democracy, and they know that the day is coming when the rest of the world will no longer need their precious oil. Yet they remain in a state of psychological denial, and they are not ready to open up and allow the sun to shine into their caves and tents—and onto the faces of their shrouded mothers and sisters.

Twisted religious belief, envy, fear, and anger have become venemous in terrorist leaders such as Osama bin Laden. If they can not, or do not know how to, create the future, they are intent on killing the future the West is creating. The result, if the fanatics have their way, will be more ages of human drudgery, sickness, misery and ignorance. In the hands of the small minority of Islamic extremists, mankind will take a giant leap backward.

There is an alternative, but it is for the fanatics to determine whether they have the courage to choose it.

The alternative is to open their eyes and tell the truth to their followers. Islamic religious leaders can save themselves and millions of their followers if they will: 1. Accept and encourage the same roles for women that exist in enlightened societies; 2. Accept the fact that people unlike them have religious values and secular ideals that must be tolerated; and 3. Agree that authoritarianism, poverty, and anti-modernist thinking must be reversed, as *New York Times* columnist Thomas Friedman has suggested.

But is it realistic to think that the fanatics' hollow promises will stop, and that the above alternative will be considered by Islamic extremists, when they have no awareness of the Enlightenment?

Another Quick Historical Refresher: The European Enlightenment

What was the European Enlightenment, and why is it such an important concept as we seek to understand Islamic fanatics?

The Enlightenment was a period in human history that had its roots in the sixteenth century, stood on the shoulders of the Italian Renaissance, and peaked at the end of the eighteenth century, when the American and French Revolutions erupted. Thomas Paine is a good example of an Enlightenment Man, and his writings, along with those of Washington, Adams, Franklin, Jefferson, Hamilton, and other American Founding Fathers, drew upon the ideas of the thinkers whose shoulders supported them.

The very name of this period, the "Enlightenment," is symbolic of the LIGHT of knowledge that education and free inquiry shined into the dark corners of human superstition and ignorance after the medieval period. This new awakening changed the world more profoundly than even the high periods of the Egyptians, the Chinese, the Arabs, the Greeks, and the Romans.

Keen observers could see the dawn of the Enlightenment when the humanist, Erasmus of Rotterdam, wrote, in the sixteenth century, that people should stop focusing totally on life after death. Erasmus argued that people should invest more of their time DOING good things for themselves and others in THIS life. His emphasis was on REASON and ACTION in this life, rather than on BELIEF in a later life.

Such a shift toward secularism, and away from the medieval obsession with religion and the afterlife, shocked most of Erasmus' contemporaries. It especially jolted the priests whose power and status revolved around the keys (that only they possessed) to Paradise. It is precisely this jolt that many fundamentalist Islamic religious leaders want to avoid today. They know what they will lose, and so do their slaves.

We seldom pause to consider the results of the Enlightenment that now serve as the foundation stones beneath our daily lives in the West. Islamic fanatics envy or fear—and do not understand—the following world-changing consequences of the Age of Reason:

• **The Enlightenment delivered its liberating and labor-saving benefits into the hands of the common man.**

The fruits of such inventions and discoveries as the steam engine, electricity, the internal combustion gasoline engine, flight, mass production, the conveyor belt, timepieces to enable precise navigation at sea, identification of germs, and inoculation against diseases such as smallpox, quickly became widespread enough *that the common man could benefit from them* to *uplift his personal life and release himself from disease and the drudgery of manual labor.* Liberation from drudgery and disease, combined with enormous increases in agricultural and industrial productivity, made it possible for a "middle class" of tradesmen (mechanics, printers, metalsmiths, electricians, pharmacists) to develop between the only two classes of medieval times—the elite and the destitute. The development of a middle class led, in turn, to enormous social changes. What were some of these changes? The broadening of the literate and educated population, the leveling of the rigid old medieval social hierarchy, the opening of hundreds of new job categories for millions of people, and a realization that the common man might be capable of governing himself.

- **The Enlightenment brought, along with its technological, medical, and industrial innovations, an anti-absolutist revolution in thinking about religion.**

Like the practical results of technology noted above that liberated Western Man and helped create a healthy middle class, the anti-absolutist revolution IN THINKING made possible the American and French revolutions and the separation of church and state in the United States. For the first time in millennia, the common man could think freely and worship freely (or worship not at all). In the eighteenth century, Thomas Paine wrote a "confession of faith" that no one would dare write in Islamic countries even today. Here is Paine's confession of religious truth as he saw it:

I believe in one God, and no more; and I hope for happiness beyond this life. I believe in the equality of man, and I believe that religious duties consist in doing justice, loving mercy, and endeavoring to make our fellow creatures happy. I do not believe in the creed professed . . . by any church that I know of. My own mind is my own church . . . . All national institutions of churches . . . appear to me no other than human inventions set up to terrify and enslave mankind and monopolize power and profit. I do not mean . . . to condemn those who believe otherwise. They have the same right to their belief as I have to mine. But it is necessary to the happiness of man that he be faithful to himself . . . . It is impossible to calculate the moral mischief . . . that mental lying has produced in society.

• The Enlightenment made law the only king in America.

The European Enlightenment, with its emphasis on Reason, put monarchy in its place, BENEATH the reasoned and democratic will of the people. The roots of this revolutionary democratic thought are traceable in Greek and Roman history, in the English Magna Carta of 1215; and in the writings of Algernon Sidney,

John Locke, and the writings of Encyclopedists such as Diderot and Voltaire. Law, the new king, concretized the four theoretical pillars of Western democratic jurisprudence:

1. There are *inalienable (natural) rights* common to all human beings that CANNOT be taken away (life, liberty, and the pursuit of happiness)

2. Government is based on a *social contract* containing reciprocal duties between the governors and the governed

3. The people have a *right to revolution* when government usurps their inalienable rights--and thus becomes tyrannical

4. To stop the accumulation of excessive power in any one part of society, there must be *checks and balances between distinctly separate branches of government*

No longer after 1787 did the common man need to hopelessly concede that he forever would be governed by people whose warlord power, bloodline pedigree, or ecclesiastical garb guaranteed their dominance. The common man, using common sense, could seriously aspire to the political leadership of his nation.

(We must remember, however, that terms such as "the common man" have not applied to every American citizen until recently. In 1787, when the Constitution was ratified, landless people,

most people of color, and women could not vote or otherwise aspire to political leadership. Many Americans whose roots reach back nearly four hundred years on this continent are still striving to make our democracy more just and equal. This still incomplete struggle for justice and equity can serve as a good lesson for those nations that seek to become democratic, free, and happy in a short time. Democracy is a never-ending process rather than a short-term goal to be achieved in the blink of an eye.)

- **The Enlightenment changed the function of public education.**

For thousands of years, education had been assigned the task of preserving the traditions of the past. With Reason in the high chair, the Enlightenment gave education a new assignment: Changing and creating the future through USEFUL KNOWLEDGE. The primary function of Western education, especially American free, universal, and compulsory public education, became teaching men and women to think analytically *in order to solve problems and improve the human condition.* No more rocking back and forth in mindless madrassas and slavishly memorizing pages full of words dictated by a ruling elite of professors and priests. No more standing at attention and reciting, verbatim, the lesson learned in the way Pavlov taught his dogs to salivate when a bell was rung. Out with classical conditioning. In with thinking.

Thomas Jefferson, the third American President, said that democracy's foundation must be laid in an educated voting public. Democracy will collapse from within, he said, if the people are ignorant. Why? Because ignorant people will not vote at all--or they will vote stupidly and as they are told by manipulators who control or pay them.

In a letter to Colonel Charles Yancey in 1816, Jefferson said, "If a nation expects to be ignorant and free, in a state of civilization, it expects what never was and never will be."

Another Founding Father of America, Benjamin Franklin, advised, and American educators endorsed, the following: "Work hard, be diligent, seize opportunities, be honest but not too intellectual. . . . We are not born to be what we become." Franklin and Jefferson knew that education can change us for the better-- as long as we are free to HOPE, to DREAM, and as long as we are FREE TO ACHIEVE.

In the context of this book, and its title, *Common Sense Rediscovered*, it is noteworthy that Franklin warned about the danger of becoming "too intellectual." Like the millions of Americans who would follow him, Benjamin Franklin emphasized the value of being PRACTICAL in the new world, and leaving excessive intellectualism to those elitists who TALK endlessly but never DO anything.

The West's notion of thinking analytically and freely is frightening to many of today's Islamic fundamentalists, and to all of today's Islamic fanatics. Leaders of Al Quaeda, Hamas, the Taliban, and other fanatical movements want their students to dwell in the past, where their thoughts will be neatly circumscribed by ancient taboos and imperatives.

Why?

Because freethought poses an enormous threat to the *power* of the Islamic ruling elite.

These rulers continue to ride on the backs of their fearful underlings, and they keep them in mental slavery by USING their schools to preserve ignorance and stifle natural curiosity and reason. Girls in some extremist Islamic communities are not allowed to attend school. As a result, at least half of the population is locked into the most vile ignorance and superstition. Tragically, the potential of millions of women for controlling disease, guaranteeing clean drinking water, and harnessing human curiosity and achievement is nullified by an educational system that says "females are insignificant as thinkers and activists in society."

The Enlightenment and America

An incalculably important coincidence took place when a new physical world opened just as the Enlightenment came to full bloom. The New World, America, came to be the PERFECT bed in which to plant the seeds of Enlightenment thought. The soil in the New World was not tainted with histories to be lived down. There were no ancient and unsettled blood feuds between families and clans, no infestations of tangled power elites, and no social classes that would or could not speak to each other.

To the contrary, the American frontier was full of virgin land, fresh and unploughed. Frontiersmen mingled, intermarried, depended on each other for survival, and reflexively replaced the noun "servant" with the NEW and more egalitarian noun "help."

Bring on the liberating seed of the Enlightenment, said Thomas Paine in 1776: Its common sense will flourish here!

And behold: Paine was right. Listen to what an early American immigrant said about the new mentality in America as he looked back on the Old World, where most European emigrants had owned absolutely nothing, including their own thoughts.

Michel-Guillaume De Crevecoeur, an American colonist from France, asked, in the mid-eighteenth century, the simple question, "What is an American, this new man?"

He then answered his own question.

(The American) is either an European or the descendant of an European; hence that strange mixture of blood, which you will find in no other country. I could point out to you a man, whose grandfather was an Englishman, whose wife was Dutch, whose son married a French woman, and whose present four sons have now four wives of different nations. He is an American, who, leaving behind him all his ancient prejudices and manners, receives new ones from the new mode of life he has embraced, the new government he obeys, and the new rank he holds. He becomes an American by being received in the broad lap of our great Alma Mater. . . Here individuals of all nations are melted into a new race of men, whose labours and posterity will one day cause great change in the world. Americans are the western pilgrims, who are carrying along with them that great mass of arts, sciences, vigour, and industry, which began long since in the east; they will finish the great circle. The Americans were once scattered all over Europe; here they are incorporated into one of the finest systems of population which has ever appeared . . . . Here the rewards of his industry follow with equal steps the progress of his labour; his labour is founded on the basis of nature, self-interest; can it want a stronger allurement? Wives and children, who before in vain demanded of him a morsel of bread, now, fat and frolicsome, gladly help

their father to clear those fields whence exuberant crops are to arise to feed and to clothe them all; without any part being claimed, either by a despotic prince, a rich abbot, or a mighty lord. Here religion demands but little of him; a small voluntary salary to the minister, and gratitude to God; can he refuse these? The American is a new man, who acts upon new principles; he must therefore entertain new ideas, and form new opinions. From involuntary idleness, servile dependence, penury, and useless labour, he has passed to toils of a very different nature, rewarded by ample subsistence. —This is an American.

In the two hundred and fifty years since Crevecoeur asked and answered his own question, the United States has produced a "race" that is more mixed by far than it was prior to our Revolutionary War, when Crevecoeur wrote of our exclusively European bloodlines. The process of mixing has been an enormous challenge to the United States, but few nations have demonstrated even half of our commitment to softening the sharp edges of race, ethnicity, and gender.

One key to the success of American demographic diversity has been the willingness of most immigrants to leave their pasts behind them, embrace the ideals of America, and *assimilate completely.*

As Crevecoeur so rightly observed, immigrants adopt America, America adopts them, and they *become*

Americans. Our short history has shown that even when such powerful physical features as skin color slow the process, assimilation CAN be accomplished, and we all can be enriched as we debate in the Grand American Forum that is comprised of the best minds from around the globe.

After paying American taxes; building a house; learning that bribes dishonor both the giver and the taker; and learning that hard work, honesty, and a positive attitude are the fundamental qualities that lead to success in America, millions of European and non-European immigrants to the New World have come to understand Crevecoeur's message.

What is Crevecoeur's message?

It is this: The past is the past, and in America, we MAKE THE FUTURE with our own hands and our own heads. There is dignity in respecting one's roots, but a person can respect his roots while becoming part of something new and better.

Islamic fanatics and men and women in a hundred slavish nations around the world have utterly no concept of America's willingness to mix and blend. Nor do they understand our irresistible optimism and HOPE. For them, most of life is dark and cynical—something to be *suffered* through, as in ages past.

They repeat their mandatory slogan every morning, as did the Soviets in the 1940s and 1950s: "I am ready for labor and struggle, and Stalin is our father."

Consequences

The development of a worldview based on Reason and the Enlightenment did not come easily. Those who contributed most to the European Enlightenment often paid a high price for their revolutionary thinking. Martin Luther, for example, was excommunicated by the church he loved, and he paid dearly during the rest of his life for starting the defining civil war among Christian sects in the West.

Galileo was nearly executed, and the Roman Church made him recant for proving that the earth revolves around the sun.

Hundreds of thousands of men and women paid with their lives in the European witch hunts and religious pogroms that burned people at the stake, drowned them, and drove them to the New World so they could be free from absolutism in all its forms.

Algernon Sidney came to be called "Sidney the Martyr" because he went to the scaffold in England for writing, in his book, *Discourses Concerning Government*, that "the Liberties of Nations are from God and Nature, not from Kings." At a time when the kings of Spain, France, and Sweden had inherited their crowns

IN INFANCY, Algernon Sidney also wrote, "The rigour of the Law is to be temper'd by men of known integrity and judgment, and not by the Prince who may be ignorant or vicious." Sidney's ideas influenced John Locke, and Sidney was Thomas Jefferson's chief mentor.

Jefferson nearly paid with his own life when the British arrived at his beloved home, Monticello, just hours after he had fled the certain death that would have been his punishment for treason.

(Few Americans today realize that the punishment for treason faced by all of the American Founding Fathers during the Revolutionary War was extraordinary. It consisted of the following, as stated by a sentencing judge to some Irish rebels: "You are to be drawn on hurdles to the place of execution, where you are to be hanged by the neck, but not until you are dead; for, while you are still living your bodies are to be taken down, your bowels torn out and burned before your faces, your heads then cut off, and your bodies divided each into four quarters, and your heads and quarters to be then at the King's disposal; and may the Almighty god have mercy on your souls.")

As we consider the perspective of those who now call us "infidels," we must remind ourselves, as mentioned earlier, that most lower-class people in Islamic nations *believe what they are told to believe.*

It is not surprising that when the bearded head mullah shouts "infidel," all of the sheep in the herd bleat the same thing. For truth, the sheep know, comes not from their own thoughts; it comes from the ram of the herd. He knows best. He always has. And he always will. For that is *the way things are* outside the legacy of the Enlightenment.

George Washington, the first President of the United States, stated that the safety and happiness of the governed are the first two duties of government.

How many national and tribal leaders today embrace such a selfless idea? Sadly, most national and tribal leaders continue to place THEMSELVES first, and their citizens second.

Of all nations on Earth, the United States has been looked to by more people than any other as the country where human happiness has been achieved. Was George Washington right in believing that general happiness can be achieved among citizens of a free nation? Is it possible to measure progress toward such an amorphous goal?

In an effort to answer this question, let us look at the results of an attitude poll of the American population. The survey was conducted in August 1994 by the Roper Center for Public Opinion at the University of Connecticut. Here are the results:

• 80% said they are completely or substantially happy with both their jobs and their lives

- 70% said they are where they should be in their jobs, based on their talents and the effort they put forth on the job
- 85% said their home lives are wonderful or pretty good
- 74% said hard work is the key to getting ahead in the U.S.
- 80% said the U.S. is still the best place to live in the world
- 50% said they are involved in volunteer work to help others

Such a poll takes on additional significance when we consider that the first collection and analysis of public opinion ever in the former Soviet Union could not take place until 1989. The above Roper Center survey results become even more compelling when we ask what might be the result of a similar poll taken today in Somalia, Iran, North Korea, Sudan, Liberia, Nigeria, or a dozen other nations where monarchs, warlords, or the Party gerontocracy rule in order to maintain happiness for THEMSELVES, rather than their citizens.

Would such a poll even be allowed in these countries?

Are there enough literate citizens in such nations to fill out a questionnaire?

Are people near enough to a functioning telephone to respond to a person conducting a telephone survey?

Would the citizens dare speak openly and honestly, or would they do as people have done under repressive political and religious regimes throughout history— think one thing, say another, and do yet another?

More Consequences—And Possibilities

In addition to missing the opportunity for widespread happiness, what else did the Islamic fanatics miss when the Enlightenment passed them by?

They missed so much scientific research in medicine that today their sheikhs, emirs, sultans, imams, and mullahs travel to England, Germany, Switzerland, and the United States to have their heart bypass surgeries, brain surgeries, cancer treatments, hip replacements, and facelifts.

They missed so much advancement in education that they send their sons to England, Germany, and the United States to attend college and university.

They missed so much technological development that they send the sons and daughters of their "lower class" citizens to the aviation and technical schools, and community colleges, in England, Germany, and the United States in order to keep their fleets of American and European-built jet airplanes flying safely.

They missed so much of the development of self-governance that they sit on the sharp edge of their own swords, delicately balancing the percentage of their own population that they can trust against the percentage of guest workers they import at low wages from Pakistan, India, Sri Lanka, the Philippines, and Bangladesh. These "guest workers" do the work to which their own citizens will not stoop.

Finally, they missed so much tolerance for secular and religious diversity that they must turn a blind eye and pretend to be religiously pure while their sons sneak off in sleek jets with pockets full of oil money for sex weekends in Bangkok.

Reverse the Intellectual Diaspora of the Jews?

Israel is a hybrid slice of Middle Eastern and Western culture inserted into the midst of the Islamic world. The Jews left the Middle East, and millions of them lived in the West long enough to absorb the legacy of the European Enlightenment. In 1948, and in the years since 1948, Jews have returned to what they claim as their Biblical homeland. These Israelis have insights that some of their more provincial Islamic neighbors have missed completely.

Perhaps a question should be put to Jews in Israel by the Moslems in the Middle East: "What did you learn during your Diaspora that has enabled you to develop a functional democracy and a government based on the rule of law, rather than on the rule of warlords or religious elites?"

If such a question were to be honestly asked, and honestly answered, a first step toward peace might be taken in the modern Middle East. By asking such questions, not only of Israelis, but also of Western Europeans and Americans, fundamentalist Islamic leaders might come to better understand the legacy of the Enlightenment—and more wisely decide what *parts* of that legacy they want to incorporate into their culture--or reject.

On April 29, 1993, a progressive Arab Sheikh in the United Arab Emirates and I sat together in his palace in Abu Dhabi. It was evident that he wanted to INCORPORATE some (but not all) Western educational ideas into his nation's educational system. At his invitation I was serving as co-chair of an international team that was completing an accreditation review of one of his technical colleges. His hunting falcons were visible in their falconry outside the window over his right shoulder, and his office walls were covered with pistols, rifles, knives, and swords.

His Excellency, Sheikh Nahayan bin Mubarak al Nahayan, raised his finger, teacher-like, and said, "Someday, the West will not need our oil. It is my duty as a leader to plan for the future and provide my people with a strong and independent system of primary, secondary, and higher education. If they have a good education, they will never have to return to the camels and the wandering life of my Bedouin grandfathers. I have rented your brain, Professor Herder, to help us make sure our higher education system has integrity and will serve our citizens well."

Progressive leaders such as Sheikh Nahayan understand the wisdom of creating a balance between his traditional culture and the modern world. A "blend" is a worthy goal, even if the process of blending is difficult. Americans can testify to the difficulty—and the rewards—of the effort. As the motto of the United Negro College Fund says in the United States, "A human mind is a terrible thing to waste." If we learn to blend peacefully, we can leverage the genius of many minds and perspectives.

SUMMARY

Islamic fundamentalists, and especially the fanatics, are entering the twenty-first century with a clear understanding that they have been left out of the world's decision-making process. They also have realized that they are valued only for the black mineral beneath the surface of their deserts, rather than for their intelligence and the once-brilliant culture they shared with the West when it was shrouded in darkness and ignorance. When we wonder why the

9/11 attack took place, we should not be surprised that many Arabs are jealous, frightened, and angry.

Lack of meaningful employment in the Middle East, Africa, and the Southeast Asian Subcontinent has left millions of people adrift. And as the electronic global village has provided a computerized and televised view of the lifestyle of the wealthy West, with real jobs for nearly everyone, Islamic jealousy, fear, and anger have turned to desperation and rage.

Because conservative Islam cannot change the future to conform to its own absolutist ideals, and because many Islamic fundamentalist leaders are unwilling to consider balancing traditional culture with participation in the modern world, a decision has been made to DESTROY the future that the dominant West is creating.

After numerous terrorist attacks against Western targets around the world in the past two decades, Islamic Fundamentalists finally hit America precisely between the eyes on September 11, 2001.

Thomas Jefferson said, in 1786, "If the happiness of the mass of the people can be secured at the expense of a little tempest now and then, or even of a little blood, it will be a precious purchase."

As if in response to Jefferson, the 9/11 attack was tragically tempestuous and bloody.

The people on the four planes that crashed in the U.S. on 9/11 were not martyrs. They were unwilling and unknowing symbols. They had plans, they had hopes, and, like people everywhere, they wanted to simply live in peace and happiness.

It was not their intent, and it was not their choice, that their blood should mingle with the blood of other free men and women who have paid down the debt incurred in this "precious purchase" for all mankind.

Their blood begs a question that must be answered by all Americans and our allies in the West: Are we fully committed to the ideals upon which human freedom is founded? Are we prepared to do everything necessary to maintain these ideals?

Everything necessary? Everything?

Is it too harsh to apply Thomas Paine's words to ourselves today? Here is what he said in *Common Sense*: "If . . . you can . . . pass [this violation] over, then I ask, Hath your house been burnt? Hath your property been destroyed before your face? Are your wife and children destitute of a bed to lie on, or bread to live on? Have you lost a parent or child by their hands, and yourself the ruined and wretched survivor? If you have not, then you are not a judge of those who have. But if you have, and still can shake hands with the murderers, then you are unworthy the name of husband, father, friend, or lover, and whatever may be your rank or title in life, you have the heart of a coward, and the spirit of a sycophant."

Chapter III

Ten Lessons That Can Lead to Action

Wise people search for lessons in every tragedy and every failure.

In Chapter II, we attempted to understand the terrorists and their motives. Before we consider some specific lessons the 9/11 attack can teach, let us take a moment to paint the background against which the lessons will be highlighted.

There were two reasons why America was named the "New World" after Christopher Columbus' famous voyage across the Atlantic in 1492. The first reason was, obviously, the NEWNESS of everything in America that awaited discovery.

The second reason, distance, was nearly as important, for the New World could have been called the "Distant World." It was much farther away in European, Asian, and African imaginations of the fifteenth century, than the Moon is in our minds today.

America was literally OCEANS away. Months away by sailing vessels. A *lifetime* away if the seas showed their teeth—or if one were thrown overboard because he was slave cargo when rations became short on a vessel becalmed in the doldrums.

But today, especially since the fanatics' attack on the United States, the world has shrunk.

The global village about which Marshall McLuhan wrote in 1968 has become the starkest sort of reality, and our east, south and west coasts are virtually contiguous with the borders of Yemen, Iraq, Iran, Pakistan, and Saudi Arabia. The result is that our enemies can cross our borders electronically in nanoseconds, and they can cross our borders physically, with weapons and destructive plans, within days or hours.

Americans no longer are invulnerable on their remote island protected by the Pacific and Atlantic Oceans, and we no longer can afford to remain naïve. We no longer dare to ignore what goes on elsewhere in the world.

Gone is the luxury of feeling secure in the belief that we are loved by all of those to whom we have sent food, money, and medicine. Gone are the days when we could feel secure in the belief that people in other lands remember and thank us for having had our fathers and grandfathers drafted into military service in order to free them from tyrants such as Adolph Hitler and Benito Mussolini.

If we are to understand fully the lessons that the 9/11 attack can teach, Americans must try to see ourselves against a humbling global backdrop, not just against the backdrop of what we formerly thought of as a huge island continent. To help us gain this perspective, let us listen to an excellent teacher who has eyes different than our own.

In a speech given to Fulbright Association Alumni at their Annual Conference in Washington, D.C., on October 3, 1997, Vaclav Havel, poet, writer, philosopher, and President of the Czech Republic, characterized the United States as he sees our country. His are the eyes of a man who grew up in the East, not the West. He hungered, struggled, and was imprisoned for dreaming that he might someday freely embrace the ideals upon which the United States is founded. Here are his words:

I believe that, for the rest of the world contemporary America is an almost symbolic concentration of all the good and bad of our civilization - ranging from the fantastic development of science and technology generating more welfare and profundity of civil liberty and strength of democratic institutions, to the blind cult of perpetual economic growth and never-ending consumption, no matter how detrimental to the environment, the dictates of materialism, consumerism and advertising, the voiding of human uniqueness and its replacement by the uniformity of the round-the-clock noise of TV banality.

For these reasons, the way in which America will assume its responsibility for the world should embody those premises which alone have a chance of saving this civilization as a whole: this way should be imbued with new spirituality, a new ethos and new ethics, hence exactly with the things that should be adopted by all cultures, all spheres of civilization and all nations of today's world as a condition of their very survival.

Taking into consideration the fact that our planet has shrunk profoundly, and taking into consideration the "outside" perspective of a philosopher-statesman as widely respected as Vaclav Havel, what lessons should Americans learn as a result of the Islamic terrorist attack?

Lesson 1—America's Ideals and Morality ARE America

President Havel's observations echo those of Thomas Paine in *Common Sense*. According to Havel, the cause of America is STILL "in a great measure the cause of all mankind." The spirituality, ethos, and ethics of the United States CAN make a difference. This is especially true as cynicism and doubt about U.S. values and behavior have become more common around the world--and as some good people question whether the

United States will wear with dignity and wisdom its mantel as the only superpower on Earth.

Our cause has worked like a magnet to attract millions of asylum-seekers across American borders in the past three hundred years. The attraction continues, and the American Dream is still very much alive. Ships and small boats from China, Haiti, and Cuba frequently are crashed into American beaches by their captains so people can leap ashore to escape terror and ignorance in their own countries, and find freedom and hope here.

As these words are being written, tragic news stories are informing us that a large number of children near Kinshasa, in the African Congo, were buried alive or hacked to death with machetes last week because local shamans believed the children, who had AIDS, were bewitched. Almost as tragically, in Islamic nations throughout the Middle East, North Africa, and Southeast Asia, the death penalty awaits anyone who converts from a belief in Allah.

According to a recent newspaper report, "An Islamic court overturned the conviction of an illiterate mother sentenced to be stoned to death for having sex out of wedlock." Questions and criticism from around the world created pressure on the Nigerian court that eventually spared the young woman's life. The young mother, Amina Lawal, held her two-year-old baby while Judge Ibrahim Mai-Unguwa read the court's opinion that there were procedural errors leading to the original decision. Ms. Lawal had divorced her husband two years before giving birth. Judge Unguwa noted that according to some interpretations of Shariah (strict Islamic law), babies can remain in their mothers' wombs for more than five years. This made it possible that her ex-husband could have impregnated her before the divorce.

If these primitive acts and notions still exist in the year 2003, is it any wonder that people seek asylum in the United States and other free nations in order to escape domination by the powerful, cunning, and ignorant leaders of their own tribes and nations?

And if, as the evidence indicates, the United States is slipping rapidly into vulgarity, incivility, and arrogance, isn't it time for us to measure up and be the good moral example for the world that we once were and still can be?

The rest of the world is watching us more carefully than ever, and most of its inhabitants want something worthy to emulate.

In the final analysis, America has been respected by people around the globe not just because it is America, and not just because of the popular appeal of Hollywood films and Louis Armstrong's jazz music. America has been respected because of what it symbolized: Hope, idealism, freedom, and opportunity.

If we forget this, all will be lost.

As the Greeks and Romans knew, and as we must never forget, democracy is based on virtue.

If the citizens and leaders in a democracy are not virtuous, if they place their own selfish good above the common good of their society, their democracy will be doomed. Vaclav Havel said it plainly and well: Our survival is dependent upon our morality.

Do we have the grit and willpower to elect the most virtuous and intelligent men and women as our leaders, regardless of political correctness, race, gender, or ethnicity—and can we find men and women who possess such moral *gravitas*?

Do our judges have the grit and willpower to sentence to life those corporate executives whose lying and stealing are traitorous acts that undermine our freedom and survival?

Do we have the grit and willpower to break up the monopoly on news and "truth" that media conglomerates now have?

Are we selfless enough to change our laws and behavior so we stop siphoning off far more than our share of the world's natural resources?

If we are humane and fundamentally moral, and if we have the courage and strength to lead, others will follow our example.

Today we see the folly of what Rudyard Kipling called "the white man's burden." It is neither the burden of any race nor the duty of a leading nation such as the United States to save the world by controlling it or imposing its will on benign cultures around the globe. An imperial America and a new colonialism are the stuff of nightmares, not dreams or duty.

But let us be clear: When the United States and its close allies are threatened by any nation or group of nations, we must and will protect our national interests and ideals by being more clever, tough, and courageous than any threatening enemy.

And let us never become militarily weak or pacifist, for brutes understand nothing but the subtle or blunt threat of force.

As Machiavelli lectured in *The Prince*, we can balance our idealism and morality with our national self-interest. We *must* do so. Careful reading of *The Prince* teaches readers that naivete is the first step to losing one's country. Weakness is the second.

To repeat: Let us lead by example, focusing on our core ideals of life, liberty, and the pursuit of happiness. If we can *discipline* ourselves to speak softly while carrying a big stick, as President Theodore Roosevelt suggested, the rest of the world might understand that we are good—but not stupid.

Such an image can ring with authenticity and quiet strength, and it can earn both respect and international support.

Lesson 2—No Sleeping On Watch

A second lesson to be learned from the 9/11 attack is that every American needs to stand his or her "watch."

Benjamin Franklin said, "The way to be safe is never to feel secure." Thomas Jefferson said, "The price of liberty is eternal vigilance." Their messages are clear: Freedom is not a gift.

What is the state of civic literacy in the United States and the free world today? Does the common man in America, England, or France understand how he became free? Has he ever thought about the depth of his civic roots? What will it take for every public school and university in the United States to teach well and meaningfully the fundamental civic values that grew out of the Enlightenment?

If our young people are to grow up and stand their watch when their time comes, they need to know about duty, honor, and service.

And they need to know *why* the penalty for sleeping on watch is death.

Is it time for us to reintroduce the word "duty" into the American vocabulary? How long has it been since this word has been uttered to our children by parents or in our popular culture? When will we again agree that it is honorable to serve our country in wartime-- and especially in peacetime in order to prevent war?

Let us end the snobbishness among our educated elite that says they are too good to serve in the military, Peace Corps, or in mental hospitals or senior citizens' homes. Let us collectively shame the selfish man or woman who says, "I can't serve in military or civilian service because I cannot afford to cut my income potential and get off my career path for two years." Shame!

When will the day come that every job interview in the United States begins with the question, "Where did you perform your two years of national volunteer service?"

In the days that immediately followed the 9/11 attack, millions of Americans and Westerners in other nations expressed amazement that such an assault had taken place. Yet there had been reports on radio, television, and in newspapers during the previous year anticipating a major attack on the United States.

The World Trade Center had already been bombed once. Six people were killed and a thousand were injured in the 1993 dress rehearsal for 9/11. But who remembers a dress rehearsal?

Who among us was alert?

Who among us was asleep?

Why were so few on watch?

Thomas Paine would have chastised us for our lack of common sense in the years and months leading to 9/11.

Now that the crisis has APPARENTLY passed, will we again become fat, dumb, and happy--and feel too secure to be safe?

Or will we grab this RARE OPPORTUNITY to reinvigorate our highest ideals and common sense?

If we are not willing to sacrifice part of ourselves for a higher cause, we must ask who will *own* the struggle in which we are engaged. Will it be only the Pentagon and the President and our men and women in uniform? God forbid.

Have we decentralized and strengthened our local food and water supply infrastructure to prevent strategic hits that can kill us by the thousands once again?

Have we taken the right steps to maintain continuity and succession of our democratically elected leaders in the event that all of Washington is destroyed by nuclear blasts?

Do we have a second seat of government ready to operate within minutes of an attack (perhaps in Canada, as planned by Churchill in 1940)? If not, will the group of surviving state governors communicate by cell phone and convene in a central location to establish martial law, print currency, collect taxes, and elect new representatives and senators who will establish a new central government?

It is not enough to be observant of dangerous behavior in potential EXTERNAL enemies. We should be frightened that voter turnout in national elections is consistently below 50% in the United States.

What is the domestic termite that keeps people in America from voting? Is it apathy? Is it civic ignorance? Are our public school teachers intelligent enough and well enough informed to make our students as eager to vote as they are to get a driver's license? Is it time to hold our elections on weekends so fewer people will be at work when they should be looking after their investment in their nation and freedom?

Now is the time, as George Washington said, for "virtuous and independent men of this country (to) come forward."

Duty calls.

Lesson 3—We Will Have to Absorb Future Hits

We learned as children, when we played King of the Hill, the old adage, "the bigger they are, the harder they fall."

The United States is now on top of the hill. And we are very big.

Nearly everyone would like to knock us off the hill or see us slip and fall because of our own clumsiness.

Why?

Because "we" are on top and "they" are not.

In the daily workplaces of the world, it is not difficult to observe a few people trying to assassinate the character of a colleague who consistently wins the Employee of the Year Award. Something in human nature seems to resent the status of those who are highly successful or who rank high in the social or economic or political pecking order. Perhaps that "something" is the primal urge to dominate, to control territory.

We, as Americans, finally need to become realists. We must never forget how many people and nations resent our status for no other reason than that it is above their own. In due time, perhaps, we will go the way of Greece and Rome.

It is increasingly clear that China is the most likely candidate to replace the United States as the leader of the world. Now is the time to ponder such a scenario—and its implications for life, liberty, and the pursuit of happiness. Has China earned the moral authority to lead? Is the United States losing its moral authority to lead? Has Henry Luce's "American Century" ended?

By definition, terrorism is unorthodox and unpredictable, and we cannot adequately guard all of our fronts and backs against its agents. What does this mean for the United States and other free nations?

Unfortunately, it means that we must be ready to ABSORB the suffering that will come with future attacks on our soil. Will all aircraft be grounded again? If so, for how long next time? Will anthrax turn up in thousands of pieces of mail across the entire nation? Have we forgotten what we experienced just a short time ago when many of us opened our mail before we brought it into the house, in order to reduce the chance that anthrax spores would enter our homes?

The wolf is at our door. And wolves, even if they are beaten back, nearly always inflict bloody wounds. The fanatics have taught us that the law of the jungle now shrieks in the treetops over our heads as it has in other nations for centuries past. Americans no longer live in Walt Disney's Fantasyland.

Do we have the stomach for what we will face next time?

Lesson 4—We Must Decide Whether Oil and Israel Are Enough to Keep Us in the Middle East

The United States has allowed itself to be drawn into the Middle East because of oil and Israel. But many Arabs are telling us to get out of their region.

We need to hear this message and think about it.

Do we *need* to be physically present, and *can we afford the costs* of being physically present, in the lands of people who want neither our companionship nor our values?

The American people should engage more fully than ever in a public debate about our role in the Middle East. And we should make sure that we hear from Middle Eastern nations and our American Arab and American Jewish citizens during the discussion, since much of their money is fueling the fire that America is expected to fight.

If Middle Eastern nations want our presence, and if the American people want us to maintain a significant presence in the Middle East, so be it. But if the signals are confusing or hesitant, or clearly negative, let us save billions of dollars and thousands of lives by redirecting our limited resources away from Israel and Palestine. Let us use our time, talent, and money to fix some of our problems at home.

With regard to oil, we can analogize the problem to a mathematical construct that everyone can understand: Let the numerator be American lives and war taxes. Let the denominator be cheap gasoline prices at the gas pump.

What is the mathematically logical result?

In the long term, are we willing to pay the price of the reckoning?

What will it take to create the *revolution in economic, political, and social values of Americans* that will enable us to think straight about our oil consumption? Are we blind? Are we as stupid as many nations think we are? As has been said about some male and female chauvinist pigs, why don't we just "get it"?

Must we be brutalized by a nuclear bomb in Washington or New York to understand the connection between terrorism and our dependence on Middle Eastern oil?

Isn't it odd that many Europeans today shut off the engines on their tiny cars every time they come to a stoplight—while many Americans leave their huge cars running in the parking lot when they stop and walk into the local hardware store for ten or fifteen minutes?

If we take off our blinders, and if we focus our efforts, we can reduce our oil consumption enough that we can be totally independent of Middle Eastern oil in five years. Forty years ago, Americans set a goal of going to the moon in a single decade. We accomplished our goal. We likewise can cut off our need for Middle Eastern oil if we make a decision to do so.

With regard to the second point, Israel, do we have the courage, and is it still possible, to engage in a public debate about weaning Israeli citizens from our financial and military dependence? Is it too late in the incessant Palestinian-Israeli slaughter to ask the United Nations to take responsibility for helping Jews and Arabs make peace with each other on the eastern end of the Mediterranean Sea?

How many Americans are weary of spending our money and our young men and women in the effort to "bring peace to the Middle East"? Do we dare take a public opinion poll on this politically incorrect question?

Compared to their respective representation in the American population, what percentage of American Jews and American Arabs serve in our American military forces? Do we dare get the facts and discuss this politically incorrect question? Who is doing the lobbying, and who is doing the fighting?

If the United States disengages from the Israeli-Palestinian mess, will all Americans be safer at home and abroad?

Why is it the task of the United States, virtually alone, to fix a blood feud that is not of our making? Does the average American understand who is paying the bill and shedding the blood in someone else's fight? Or does the Jewish-Arab fight belong to the United States alone?

Lesson 5— Fix the U.S. Immigration and Naturalization Service

If anything in American government has ever been perverse, it is the INS (Immigration and Naturalization Service-now part of the Office of Homeland Security). It is a paved and duty-free landing strip for our enemies.

Let me be clear: The United States of America is an immigrant nation, and we should not cut off the infusion of new ideas and talent completely. However, we now are under attack, and there is nothing in our

Constitution or Bill of Rights that comprises a suicide pact. We must determine how many immigrants we can absorb intelligently and seamlessly—*and we should not forget for a single minute that loyalty to the United States is a requirement for citizenship.*

Based on what we now know about the nineteen Islamic terrorists who attacked us on 9/11, some manipulated their student visa status to fulfill their murderous mission. Shortly after the attack, it became known that there were approximately a thousand illegal aliens in the United States who had exhausted their due process appeals in various hearings.

According to reports in the public media, all of these people had been ordered deported. Shockingly, this thousand men and women were not found and shipped back where they came from.

Why?

Was there a lack of money to find them? Was there a lack of will to find them? Was there a lack of organization and infrastructure to find them? Was it hoped that they might be fast-tracked into American citizenship so they could be counted on to vote for whichever political party did not hunt them down and deport them?

According to Patrick Buchanan, in *The Death of the West*, the United States deports only approximately one percent of the estimated eleven million ILLEGAL aliens who enter this country every year. Furthermore, a third of the LEGAL immigrants who come to the United States have not finished high school, and approximately 22 percent do not even have a ninth-grade education (compared to less than 5 percent of our native-born citizens). In 1980, federal and state prisons housed 9,000 criminal aliens. By 1995, federal and state prisons held 59,000.

The voice of the American people needs to be heard and paid attention to by the U.S. Immigration and Naturalization Service, and by the President and Congress. Americans are worried, and they should be, as they see our borders overrun by illegal foreigners and legal aliens who demand money, free education, free medical benefits, nonsensical "official" identity cards, drivers' licenses, and the "right" to make their native language the lingua franca of entire communities in the United States. This song can be played again, and more loudly, in Germany, England, and across Western Europe.

If the United States continues down the immigration policy path it currently is on, we Americans will end up precisely where we are headed.

Where is that place?

Perhaps that place is Denmark, where telling the truth about one's feelings regarding the influx of foreigners is an invitation to being branded a Nazi, a racist, or a xenophobe. Again according to *Death of the West*, Denmark's Interior Minister (who was a left-wing student radical during the 1960s) set off a firestorm by declaring that refugees in Denmark with criminal records should be put on a desert island. Her comment came after a series of gang rapes of Danish women by Middle Eastern immigrants, and after demands by the refugees that Danish law be changed to conform with Islamic law. The requested new law would include restrictions on women and approve cutting off limbs as punishments for theft.

Thirty-three percent of Denmark's social budget is dedicated to the four percent of the nation's population that is comprised of non-Western immigrants.

Is it time for Americans to demand monthly detailed reports in the press about the ways in which the U.S. Immigration and Naturalization Service is being reformed and restructured—with specific examples of how **action** is being taken to plug one of the largest holes in our national security?

No longer should our borders be tantalizingly inviting sieves through which criminals and terrorists can simply slosh into our nation. Half the world wants to come to America, and we have a moral and public duty to be selective. We can screen prudently without closing the door to all the world's "tired, . . . poor, . . .

huddled masses yearning to breathe free" under the protective arm of our Statue of Liberty.

For ten years, until we have listened carefully to American citizens to understand what kind of immigration policy we should have, let us "just say no" to certain people from certain places and certain clans and tribes.

It is time to write a few words in the sand with the other end of the stick that for years has written, "Yankee Go Home." Our message can be equally simple and clear: "Certain People *Stay* Home."

Who in Congress or the White House will address this issue and our current immigration law?

Lesson 6—Citizens Must Continue To Tell It Like It Is

A sixth lesson is that American citizens need to continue to speak the truth in public. In the United States, unlike some Western nations (and nearly ALL nonwestern nations), we have the remarkable and intuitive ability to take a moral position quickly, and to state it without hesitation. Although such action might appear to hundreds of other nations to be foolish or dangerous, part of the genius of this untidy and somewhat brash democratic experiment is that Americans often do what simply is *right*.

Most Americans are sufficiently sensitive to the feelings and sensibilities of fellow citizens that they will not needlessly offend them when they speak publicly about minorities, women, handicapped people, and foreign **guests** in our country. We should not be hypersensitive, however.

Thank goodness that people are demonstrating on American streets today for and against our current policy in the Middle East. They are telling it as they see it. Their voices, pro and con, are important voices, and they must be heard by our elected leaders. They also must be heard by their neighbors and by people around the world. Their protests provide heroic evidence that the blood of our forefathers—and of our neighbors on 9/11—has purchased our right to speak out, to tell it like it is.

An interesting example of people using their right to speak out was reported on (American) National Public Radio on October 18, 2002. According to the report, a group of Americans in Nevada City, California, organized a protest against the U.S. going to war in Iraq. The protest was designed to obstruct traffic, so the police informed members of the group that they would be arrested. Because Nevada City is a small town, and because the Chief of Police knew many of the protesters, he asked the leader of the protest group to simply give him a count of the number of people who were prepared to go to jail. "We want to make sure we order enough meals for everyone. While you're at it, would you please get a separate count of those who are vegetarians? We want to order the right kind of food."

How many other nations in the world treat political protesters with such respect? Our neighbors in the Middle East and around much of the unfree world find it difficult to believe that such protesters are not shot immediately—or their family members beheaded in the nearest soccer stadium.

We must guard against the social pressure of those who would manipulate us into keeping our mouths shut. The common man in the United States has not yet lost all of his common sense, and he knows that ours is ALREADY the most diverse, tolerant, and free society on earth.

We are morally bound to save this unique society, even if we must tell the chattering class of pseudo-intellectuals to back off. The common American will tell the truth most of the time, if he feels he can speak without being branded a Nazi or a racist.

Lesson 7— Three Things Are Needed to Treat the New Global Cancer: Power, Morality, and Allies

In certain circles, especially elite intellectual circles in the West, the word "power" is taboo.

Why?

Because members of such circles often equate power with arrogance, and they prefer to believe that cooperation is more important than competition as the prime mover of human progress. Darwin's observations about competition for scarce need satisfiers make many people uncomfortable.

But men and women around the *rest of the world* instinctively understand the laws of competition, and they know that Nature rewards strength, cunning, and adaptability.

A discussion of power (and Darwinian competition) is risky; some readers are so uncomfortable with both topics that they might put this text down and never pick it up again. Let us take the risk, however. We *must* address power. And we *must* talk about morality and developing strong alliances in order to defeat malignant diseases in the modern world. To do otherwise would be intellectually irresponsible after September 11, 2001.

The men and women who leaped from the top of the World Trade Center into the hideously optimistic sunlight of 9/11 understood in one terrible moment of decision what it means to lose. They would want us to talk about winning and losing, about power and weakness – and about what action we should take to cure the global cancer that stole their lives in eight rushing seconds.

The swirl of history has deposited temporary sandbars of strength in the United States, Europe, and parts of Asia. This strength, used judiciously and humanely, can help create a better future for millions of people who now are unable to think freely, speak freely, or govern themselves.

Hundreds of nations and tribes around the world *cannot* exert such influence. They are too weak to do so. Or they have never considered the possibility that they *ought* to help humankind do anything.

In light of the temporary strength deposited in a few nations today, the 9/11 attacks on New York and Washington beg the same moral question that Aristotle pondered in ancient Greece: Is there a universal moral duty to do good?

An answer to this question is offered by the Golden Rule of ten of the world's best-known religions. In slightly different words and formulations, they all state that such a duty DOES exist, and they also define what it means to "do good." Both the Judaeo-Christian and Islamic moral traditions, for example, teach their adherents *to do unto others as they would have others do unto them.* Secular philosophers such as Immanuel Kant agree. Kant urges people everywhere *always to do that which, if universalized, would benefit mankind.*

The 9/11 attack by the Islamic fanatics makes one thing bluntly clear: People who believe in reason, the rule of law, and *a moral duty to benefit mankind* are in an uphill race against the Islamic kamikazes.

If the United States and its allies do not run the uphill race, who will?

Hitler and the holocaust taught us the consequences of appeasement and looking the other way during the 1930s and 1940s. The 1994 genocide in Rwanda taught us again that inaction can be immoral. Edmund Burke said it best: "All that is necessary for the forces of evil to win in the world is for enough good men to do nothing."

Only an *alliance of strong and deeply committed nations* was able to bring down the irrational forces in Germany, Italy, and Japan during World Wars I and II. As in 1917 and 1941, it is the duty of the President and the Congress of the United States to build alliances necessary to win this latest war against irrationalism. Losing is not an alternative.

How near is the time when millions of thoughtful men and women around the globe will despair as they sit on the floor, handcuffed and clothed in an orange prisoner's robe, while their masked executioner stands behind them and unsheaths his dagger to behead them?

Will a question stick in their throats? "Why didn't we try to make the world better when we had the power to do so?"

The United States, for whatever period of strength it has left, is the world's best hope *for creating hope.* Without imposing its will on benign cultures and nations, it must fulfill its moral duty to advance scientific progress, promote human understanding and peace, and serve as a beacon for human freedom. In doing so, it must find a way to stop driving potential allies away by appearing to be arrogant. Conversely, it must find a way to *earn* the support, trust, and mutual commitment of nations that share a life-and-death stake in the outcome of our struggle against the jihadists.

There is great reason to be hopeful as we enter the twenty-first century. Despite the dark clouds of ignorance that are blowing in every direction from the Middle East, enlightened men and women in the West can summon the will to succeed in what Winston Churchill called, in 1940, "the Common Cause."

The weak, afraid, self-absorbed, and feckless nations of the world (some of them are in the West) need to see that the U.S. and its allies can and will LEAD in the effort to uplift mankind. They must see that we will not bow to those who would take us back to medieval kingdoms, primitive stonings, handchoppings, head-choppings, and kissing warlords' rings and imams' asses.

Lesson 8—Keep Our Press Free

Adhering literally to the First Amendment of the U.S. Constitution (freedom of speech and the press) is important for the security of every American every day. But it is especially important after the 9/11 attack because our freedom of speech and freedom of the press are important models for people around the world.

The tyrants of our planet, along with their willing and unwilling followers, are bound to learn something as they see us risk leaking information about our plans and our mistakes. The very fact that probing questions are ALLOWED can be instructive to those of the world who do not have freedom of speech and freedom of the press.

Last year, Russian President Vladimir Putin appeared on a National Public Radio call-in show in the United States. He responded, on the air with no delays for the purpose of editing, to all kinds of sensitive questions from average American citizens. In light of the secretive behavior of every past leader of Russia and the Soviet Union, Mr. Putin's performance was amazing. It remains to be seen whether Mr. Putin will practice such freedom of the press in Russia—or whether he will slip back into the KGB habits that shaped him and his career.

Lesson 9—Invite and Expect American Muslims To Assimilate

American Muslims, and especially American Muslim religious leaders, must lead, speak, and act more convincingly, authentically, and spontaneously in support of American ideals and the safety of American citizens. We have heard little from American Muslims since the 9/11 attack on the United States, and the silence is deafening.

Certainly, some American Muslims have helped the United States find, apprehend, and convict Muslims who are planning or actively involved in plots to damage the United States, its citizens, and its allies. But why have so many other American Muslims been so reluctant to tell what they know about the flow of money and people between the U.S. and nations where Al Quaeda and Hamas are active in planning and executing terrorist attacks against the West?

If Muslims in America are to be Americans in the sense that Crevecoeur spoke of in Chapter II, it is imperative that they disavow some of the things they said immediately after the 9/11 attack. For example, in her syndicated column on October 14, 2001, Georgie Anne Geyer quoted a Susan Sachs article in the *New York Times*. Islamic students at the Al Noor

School, in Brooklyn, New York, said, only three weeks after the 9/11 attack, "Muslims are all one. (Muslims overseas) kind of think of us as just living in America."

The students went on to say that the Koran, "'being the literal word of God,' provides the perfect blueprint for their lives, and that 'their ideal society would follow Islamic law and make no separation between religion and state.'" They added that they would support any leader "who they decided was fighting for Islam." One student "averred that he would support any Muslim whom he determined to be an observant Muslim fighting for an Islamic cause, even if it meant abandoning the United States." They told the reporter that they "would have to accept paying taxes—in order to become doctors and lawyers trained in America— but they did not like it because those taxes financed things that were un-Islamic, such as licenses for alcohol." The *Chicago Tribune* reported that some American Moslems "want to change the banking system to an Islamic one, where, for instance, interest is forbidden."

No more standing apart. American Muslims must be invited—and expected—to sit at the American table, to take nourishment with their non-Muslim neighbors, to *feel* fully like Americans—and to tell it like it is.

They are no longer in the Old World, and they need to adopt their new country if they want their new country to adopt them. If they are to be full citizens of the

United States, and if they want to help the cause of human freedom, they can and must dare to speak out. They must stop the jihadists among them who seek the downfall of the U.S. and the West. Moderate Islamic religious leaders must get control of their religion. How long will they allow their fanatical co-religionists to make a mockery of Mohammed and Allah?

Lesson 10—The United States Must Earn (Not Assume As A Right) Its Leadership Position in the World

Despite our flaws, much morality and human decency still repose in this land of opportunity.

Our American brand of morality is comprised of a combination of Puritanistic Calvinism and Greco/Roman notions about political virtue. The message of this moral mixture, to most Americans, is clear: We should fulfill our historical mission of improving the human condition.

To many, including our allies in Western Europe and the former Soviet Union, such a sense of mission appears so simplistic that it *must* be hollow and artificial.

This sense of mission is neither hollow nor artificial, and it IS what millions of Americans believe, along with our optimism and hope. We believe it deep down to the marrow of our bones.

If we combine America's moral vision and sense of mission with its size, resources, technological strength, and potential, it is reasonable to argue that the U.S. is the best and most safe repository of power and world leadership at this time.

We already have read Vaclav Havel's words about America's POTENTIAL for GOOD leadership in the world at the end of the Cold War. The task before Americans today is to ACT in such a way that we fulfill our potential to lead wisely and morally, and continue our traditional mission of uplifting mankind.

Following are plain-spoken words on this subject by a man who is less educated and less famous than President Vaclav Havel—but no less articulate. He is a farmer in New Zealand, and his name is David Ferguson.

On December 8, 1992, this author was nearly killed in an automobile accident that forced him off the main paved road that wends its way south along the coast of the Tasman Sea on the west side of the southern island of New Zealand. The truck that forced me off the road just south of Hokitika followed my swerving rental auto into a cow pasture, coming to a stop only a few yards away. After an apology by the shaken driver as he emerged from his truck, he and I struck up a conversation in his cow pasture.

Farmer Ferguson reminded me that it was Pearl Harbor Day in New Zealand. (Due to the location of the International Dateline, the Japanese bombing of Pearl Harbor on December 7, 1941, actually occurred on December 8 for New Zealanders and their neighbors in Australia and Southeast Asia.) Mr. Ferguson and I leaned against our vehicles as we speculated about the global environment after the Cold War that had ended just a year earlier, when the Soviet Union was reconstituted. Eventually, my new Kiwi friend and I exchanged names and addresses as we prepared to bid each other farewell. He then paused and asked me the following pregnant question:

"What are we going to do without you?"

Perplexed, I asked him what he meant.

He replied:

> *"Well, I'm worried about America, Mate. Your society is sliding downhill very fast, and we're worried about how long you are going to last. We now get satellite television here in New Zealand, and every day we see your crime, drugs, kids with no families, armed police with metal detectors to keep guns out of your schools, drive-by shootings.*
>
> *Your society seems to be coming apart.*

I am not only worried about you and your country; I am worried about New Zealand and the rest of the world as well. We are critical of your country, and we have been pretty hard on your nuclear submarines by not allowing them to stop in New Zealand, but we like you Americans, and we need you.

The whole world, even the United Nations, needs America for its strength and ability to keep the global picture in balance. At this moment, President Bush is sending American troops into Somalia to help starving people who are being bullied by warlords. You have no oil interests or other national interests in such a godforsaken place. It is likely that some of your boys will be killed there, yet you are going in because it is the right thing to do. Your country still acts based on moral principles and has moral authority.

I don't know what is going to happen to the rest of us when you're gone."

Mr. David Ferguson's coments, like those of Vaclav Havel, need to be heard by us.

Our challenge is NOT merely to remain in power, although Darwin, Nietzche, Ardrey (and soon Robert M. LaFollette III), and other thinkers argue convincingly that competition is innate.

Our challenge IS, however, to earn and retain the trust of other nations by what we say *and what we DO*. We must stand by our moral convictions, and when we err we must admit our mistakes, pull back, and try to set things right.

As long as we seek to balance human decency with our founding ideals and practical common sense, and as long as the United States remains an authentic metaphor for hope and freedom, this country will be ASKED to remain in a leadership position on our planet.

CONCLUDING COMMENTS ABOARD A DOOMED AIRLINER

It is September 11, 2001, and each of us in the free world is seated next to Todd Beamer, the hero of United Airlines Flight #93. Because of his heroism, and the heroism of some of our seatmates, we will crash into a Pennsylvania field a few minutes from now, rather than into the White House or the U.S. Capitol.

It is 9:45 a.m.

We have just learned through cell phone calls from our husbands and wives that three other commercial jet airliners like ours have crashed into the World Trade Center and the Pentagon.

We also know that our flight has just been hijacked, and we all have been hoping that our captors will free us when we arrive in Cuba.

Some of us realize, however, that the sun is now shining brightly through the windows on the STARBOARD side of our aircraft. Just a short time ago the sun was shining through the windows on our PORT side.

Therefore, we are now heading EAST, toward Washington, D.C., rather than WEST, toward our original destination, California.

As the thought begins to form in our minds that our hijacking might be part of a large-scale plot to destroy the White House or the Capitol Building, terrified whispers filter back to us that one of our hijackers has begun to slash the throats of people in the first class section and in the cockpit.

Our speed is accelerating, and our course is fixed.

Todd Beamer has just stood up with his cell phone still in his hand. He is uttering what a telephone operator later will report are some of his last words: "Jesus help me. Are you guys ready?"

Some of us are pacifists.

Some of us prefer dialogue and compromise over confrontation.

And the rest of us seek *common sense* solutions when we deal with a life-and-death crisis.

What will we do? What *must* we do?

Are we sunshine patriots who shrink from service to the cause of human freedom, or do we have the instinct and will to survive a wolf attack?

Will we seize the opportunity and act, or will we remain seated?

Sources

Abbreviations Used

AIP	America In Perspective: The United States Through Foreign Eyes— by Henry Steele Commager, Ed. (Random House, Inc., New York 1947)
BIP	Bobos in Paradise: The New Upper Class and How They Got There—by David Brooks (Simon and Schuster, New York 2000)
CSATC	Common Sense and The Crisis – Reproduction of edition published in 1776 by W. & T. Bradford of Philadelphia. (Dolphin Books Doubleday & Company, Inc., Garden City, New York: 1960)
DCG	Discourses Concerning Government—by Algernon Sidney (Booksellers of London and Westminster: 1698. Rare Books Collection, Michigan State University Library, East Lansing, Michigan)
DOW	Death of the West: How Dying Populations and Immigrant Invasions Imperil Our

Country and Civilization—by Patrick J. Buchanan (St. Martin's Press: New York: 2002)

FU   The Federal Union – by John D. Hicks (Houghton Mifflin Company, Cambridge: 1957)

GW   George Washington—Biography by James Thomas Flexner (Little, Brown and Company: Boston: 1970)

GPT   Giants of Political Thought: Common Sense—Thomas Paine, and The Declaration of Independence—Thomas Jefferson (Knowledge Products/Carmichael & Carmichael, Inc., Nashville: 1985)

HOW   A History of the World – by Starr, Nowell, Lyon, Stearns, and Hamerow (Rand McNally & Company, Chicago: 1960)

JA   John Adams—Biography by David McCullough (Simon & Schuster, New York: 2001)

PESC   The Protestant Ethic And The Spirit Of Capitalism – by Max Weber (Charles Scribner's Sons, New York: 1958)

RC   Roper Center for Public Opinion (University of Connecticut)

WC   Western Civilizations: Their History and
      Their Culture—by Edward McNall Burns
      (W.W. Norton & Company, Inc., New York:
      1955)

I. Thomas Paine and *Common Sense* in 1776 and 2001

Page 11   CSATC, 69

Page 14   "On October 16, 2001, Bill Moyers said" Keynote Address at the Grantmakers Association Conference—Brainerd, Minnesota, October 16, 2001 (www.grannyd.com/moyers.htm)

Page 15   "He accepted a job in the bookstore" GPT Common Sense

Page 16   "Only about a third" JA, 90

Page 17   "We were blind" GPT Common Sense

Page 18   "Plain and compelling arguments" CSATC

Page 24   "Less than a month before" JA, 117

II. Understanding the Terrorists and the 9/11 Attack

Page 29   *"In 1698, Algernon Sidney" DCG, 440*

Page 36   *"The Enlightenment was a period" WC,*
                 475-482; HOW, 193-236

Page 36   *"Keen observers could see the dawn" HOW,*
                 54, 129; WC, 369-70

Page 39   *"I believe in one God" FU, 245*

Page 40   *"Law, the new king" GPT, The Declaration*
                 of Independence

Page 42   *"Work hard, be diligent" BIP, 73*

Page 45   *"(The American) is either an European"*
                 AIP, 23

Page 48   *"Algernon Sidney came to be called" DCG,*
                 242, 354

Page 49   "(Few Americans today realize . . .)" GW
                 Vol. II, 14

Page 50   "George Washington, the first President"
                 GW Vol. III, 143

Page 50   "In an effort to answer this question" Survey
                 by Reader's Digest. Methodology: Conducted
                 by Institute for Social Inquiry/Roper Center,
                 University of Connecticut, August 22-August
                 29, 1994.   (ropercenter.uconn.edu)

Page 56   "Thomas Jefferson said in 1786" Civic
                 Literacy Resources
                 http://www.libertynet.org/edcivic/civlittr.html

Page 57   "Here is what (Paine) said in Common
                 Sense" CSATC, 33

III. Ten Lessons That Can Lead To Action

Page 61   *"I believe that, for the rest of the world"*
Speech by President Vaclav Havel on October
3, 1977, to Fulbright Association Annual
Conference in Washington, D.C. Author
was in attendance.

Page 63   *"According to a recent newspaper report"*
Lansing (Michigan) State Journal, September
26, 2003

Page 77   *"According to Patrick Buchanan" DOW,*
141-142

Page 78   *"Perhaps that place is Denmark" DOW,*
209-210

Page 88   *"For example, in her syndicated column"*
Lansing (Michigan) State Journal, October
14, 2001